AN AUTHENTIC LIFE

T0191356

AN AUTHENTIC LIFE
JENNIFER CHANG

COPPER CANYON PRESS
PORT TOWNSEND, WASHINGTON

Cover art: Sarah McKenzie, *Isolation Cell,* 2023. Oil and acrylic on wood panel, 14 × 11 in.

Copper Canyon Press is in residence at Fort Worden State Park in Port Townsend, Washington, under the auspices of Centrum. Centrum is a gathering place for artists and creative thinkers from around the world, students of all ages and backgrounds, and audiences seeking extraordinary cultural enrichment.

LIBRARY OF CONGRESS CATALOGING-IN-PUBLICATION DATA
Names: Chang, Jennifer, 1976– author.
Title: An authentic life / Jennifer Chang.
Other titles: Authentic life (Compilation)
Description: Port Townsend, Washington : Copper Canyon Press, 2024. |
  Summary: "A collection of poems by Jennifer Chang" — Provided by
  publisher.
Identifiers: LCCN 2024011019 (print) | LCCN 2024011020 (ebook) |
  ISBN 9781556596995 (paperback) | ISBN 9781619323049 (epub)
Subjects: LCGFT: Poetry.
Classification: LCC PS3603.H3573 A98 2024 (print) |
  LCC PS3603.H3573 (ebook) | DDC 811/.6—dc23/eng/20240308
LC record available at https://lccn.loc.gov/2024011019
LC ebook record available at https://lccn.loc.gov/2024011020

9 8 7 6 5 4 3 2 FIRST PRINTING

COPPER CANYON PRESS
Post Office Box 271
Port Townsend, Washington 98368
www.coppercanyonpress.org

Acknowledgments

Grateful acknowledgment is made to the editors and staffs of the publications in which these poems first appeared: *The American Poetry Review, The Believer, Cherry Tree, The Georgia Review, The Kenyon Review, Poetry, Poetry Northwest, A Public Space, Southern Indiana Review, Switchyard,* and *The Yale Review.* "The Innocent" was reprinted in *The Best American Poetry 2022* and "An Essay on War" was reprinted in *The Pushcart Prize XLVII: Best of the Small Presses 2023 Edition.* "Dialogues (Against Literature)" and "The Age of Unreason" were awarded the 2023 Levinson Prize by the Poetry Foundation. "What Is Truth" was featured on the website of the Smithsonian Asian Pacific American Center.

I am grateful for fellowships from the Elizabeth Murray Artist Residency program, Virginia Center for the Creative Arts, Hewnoaks Artist Colony, and MacDowell: each provided critical support in the form of time, space, and community. I am grateful to the George Washington University, the University of Houston, the Bennington Writing Seminars, and the University of Texas at Austin for supporting me intellectually and materially during the years I worked on this book.

Thank you to the staff of Copper Canyon Press for their tireless, passionate, and exuberant support of poetry, this book included. I'm especially grateful to Michael Wiegers, whose deep respect and care led me to trust myself more fully.

Thank you to Sarah McKenzie for the painting that graces this book's cover and for the conversations that emboldened me to see the truths behind these poems.

I am grateful to the friends who read the manuscript in various forms of completion and helped me find my way: Oliver Baez Bendorf, Lindsay Bernal, Gabrielle Calvocoressi, Jenny Johnson, Christopher Kondrich, Jennifer Kronovet, Joseph Legaspi, Tomás Morín, Kelly Nguyen, Cecily Parks, Mary Szybist, Jane Wong, and Mark Wunderlich.

Thank you to Maud Casey, whose friendship provided incubation for many of the thoughts and feelings that became many of these poems.

Thank you to the Spaars and Matsuno-Spaars for keeping me close even when I've wandered so far away, and to the McKeevers for giving me time and for loving my children (and me) so thoroughly. Thank you to the staff of *New England Review* for giving me another nest to dwell in. Thank you to my neighbors in Mount Pleasant, the best neighbors in the world. Thank you to Vievee Francis and Matthew Olzmann for taking me in right before the last stretch. Thank you to Lily Wong and Yan Zheng, whose basement I finally finished this in.

Thank you to my brother in language and spirit, Daniel DeWispelare, for being on the other side of these poems. I will miss you for the rest of my life.

My parents believe in me even when I bewilder them, and for that I am forever grateful, and my heartfelt gratitude goes to Constance Chang and Nicholas Friesner (and Clementine and Dexter).

Every day there is our Coven—thank you, witches, for sharing your witchy secrets with me and for giving me the courage to go on (and on). Let's meet later by the creek!

Everything begins and ends with the family I choose every day. My gratitude to Evan Rhodes and our children comes from the heart's deep core and, like my love for you, is boundless. I could not have dared such darkness had I not the daily promise of your light.

for Hank and Desmond

I soon realized that poets do not compose their poems with knowledge

SOCRATES IN PLATO'S *APOLOGY*

Not knowing is most intimate.

BUDDHIST KOAN

CONTENTS

AN AUTHENTIC LIFE

ONE

The Poem of Force

. . . between the impulse and the act, the tiny interval that is reflection.

Simone Weil, "The *Iliad,* or the Poem of Force"

What is that man doing?
He has been crouched in that corner for an eternity,
eight minutes, likely an hour, his gray face expressionless and
shimmering from the shallow water, the silver rim
of his glasses another prick of light
quilting the ripples rowdy children make
as they thrash and play.

I'm teaching my son how to swim today.
From the edge, he charges
at me. Why, I ask,
does the swim coach call it "charge"
and not "levitate" or "bloom"?
Again and again, I catch his attack; he laughs.

And there's that man
gazing into the space
between us, a window
onto somewhere else, not here
in the practice pool,
where children learn to tread,
to freestyle, butterfly, plunge,
and count their breaths.
Can you touch the floor?
asks my son, and down he goes
before I can say No:
without my goggles,
                              it hurts
my eyes to see underwater, the chlorine stings,
the crowd of bodies, undulating

like sudden smoke. I love to swim
because I love the warp and woof
of a good breaststroke, kicking the water
till it's waves, waving
hello, farewell,
my child's bursting the surface like fish
panicking oxygen. Even inside, the air

is sticky with summer sweat, the thrill
of not drowning, almost drowning,
not today, when the stillness
of that man in the corner
grows louder, he's here, still here, now
a ubiquity like war. Is it strange
to think of war? Strange to say it hurts

me to see him there? Or say I'm hurting him,
as if we were brothers
in the same distress, as the commotion
of children swallows all silence, their light
tossed up, tossed out, the weird elation
of their bodies raging. The violence

my mind inflicts
kills him again
and again for vexing what's merely
municipal, this center
of recreation that's neither mine nor his
alone.

        We're all pretending

the pool's our ocean . . .

how does a body take the undertow

what is under my toe, Mama

who's to say stillness isn't a sound

it may not be true

to look is not to act

who's to say

to float and drift to love the water's cold brutality and be a heat writhing through

I'm afraid

I'm not afraid of anything . . . I stared

at the Pacific—and all the children

looked at each other with a wild surmise—

Silent, upon a peak in . . .

In the Middle of My Life

I'm nobody's child, I write my father
        and lie the next day
to a friend on the phone a time

        zone away: *I'm fine.* I used to write
letters to everyone I loved; now
        I head for the woods, phone

in hand. My friend, with whom
        a decade ago I'd exchange
heartaches, each one stamped

        with exacting artlessness—writing
letters about other letters, we marveled
        how our words arrived wherever

we weren't, signed Yours Love Soon, across
        the Atlantic over the hardly blue
Blue Ridge beyond basins of western

        plains. I once loved a man
who'd force the weight of his body
        into a felt-tip pen, scoring torn

paper with savage loops of cursive.
        He wrote everything down—
whirling manifestos, treatises overtaking

        oceans of thought. In person,
he could not stop talking,
        and loudly,

louder, arms sweeping away
        the air, what I wanted to say,
an animal voice I often found

abhorrent, though
wasn't I the animal, enraged
        that being together

was nothing
        like our letters? Those accordant
silences, sweet hectic

        grappling for words. I remember
the longing inside my head,
        his beautiful letters,

mine, my fingers tracing the ridges
        of consonants, questions
and postscripts littering margins,

        uncontainable form, the page
a stage for candor. *To know another
        is the terrible work of love,*

is it not? Who said that? I note the clouds,
        see through tree canopy, late
summer, a bowl of black plums

        on the kitchen table
awaiting my return. I am walking
        up a steep hill

in the forest along a city
        parkway: what you hear is
my breathing, the roar

        of midday traffic, trees
moaning in sudden strong
        wind. It is too late

in the season for flowers,
        but there are wild herbs
with tiny white blooms,

        the truculence of fungus
newly sprung and
        plentiful after last week's rain.

My friend's trail is drier,
        unnamed, and ornery
from Texas sun. *Go ahead,*

        we each say to the other
when our voices tangle.
        It's 100° out. Writing

has no voice
        because voice is a metaphor,
I know, having read *How*

        Poems Get Made. Longenbach
calls it a "perceiving
        sensibility" that lets us pretend

—*Near 90 here*—someone is talking
        to us, "a wish
for visceral immediacy,"

        listen:
no one is here,
        the voice in my head

I thought I loved,
        merely clean syntax
and generous diction. Of that man,

"I" might have said, "as I loved
nobody, nobody loved me"—that figure,
          which is and is not me,

which was me, perhaps will be me.
          I don't particularly like writing
in the first person, in the future tense,

          though pleasures abound.
Eventually, I will not have to wait
          for my father

to come home again. I will not
          have to avoid the question
"And how is your family?" It will not

          always hurt—*Are you
by the creek?*—being his daughter.
          Yes, but it's so dry

this could be Texas.
          I don't know why
I hurt. *I wish!* And

          here is where we,
our voices, rest. I see
          an oak's roots twisted,

exposed where the hill's eroded
          from too much rain.
Everything's weather,

          I want to say, but how
I mean that voice,
          who knows. In letters

I'll never send my father,
        I number days
of drought and flood, this August's

        manic squalls bursting sewers
beyond capacity, city blocks
        gone riverine

for one night, two. Today the air's
        stiff with thirst, my marigolds
unplucked and dying, the other

yellow annuals, stiff-
        stemmed in a glorious green pot,
not a leaf left, bought

to look at, not to care for, how
        careless of me
not even to remember

        their names. *Write*
what you can't say, long-told
        advice told again: I'm nobody

to my father, and he's nobody
        to me. Do you hear that? The wish
for such visceral immediacy.

What Is Music

She told me a story about a boy,
the child of a cousin, who had not
fared well. How the conversation veered
here
                    I can't recall. I had shifted
my embouchure, butchering Varèse
as I again dashed ahead
of the metronome. That I
would never be a great flutist
was her tragedy and not mine,
it would take me years
to realize. First chair
in a minor ensemble, she fixed
her blue gaze on me
with no expression, listening
for what she once called
my pure tone
when deciding whether I was worth teaching. In the afternoon light
of her living room I paused when she sighed
a melody I could not reach,
her voice a second golden instrument,
then digressed, sparked
by a sudden shade of white
evoking summers on the Upper Peninsula,
the children wild with moss
and lake water.
                    The room where it happened
had a view
and a wall of books
that sometimes, in the dark, looked like ladders,
sometimes a row of shoulders,
men colluding. Before the accident,
the boy was the first to dive in, first
to dock his kayak, first to toss down dinner

and dart from the house, and now,
that day, he scaled the shelves
like a chased animal. One cried STOP
another WAIT, and then
a noise, a low moan that swiftly
gathered in the wood, a kind of rondo
sounding like horses
stampeding,
my teacher said, her flute across her lap,
mine leaning tiredly at my neck,
a habit I'd acquired in rehearsals
as violins usurped, once again,
the concerto's compulsion. Even after
the shelves collapsed
books kept falling, the last
colts galloping

      after the dust of elders—
ordinary stallions, old tireless
mares, clouds we all traverse
just to keep up. Never the same again, she sang,
but he survived, and we were, for a while, glad
for this new quiet, the next year
on the lake, when he'd avoid
that room and make of lake-wading
an occasional breaststroke, gently, not even reaching
the easy cove we'd measure as a lap. The worst
can happen and not be
that bad, I think she meant to say,
though perhaps thinking back
was how she endured our lessons.
The stories she told
were of other people's misfortune,
that without the expected glory
the boy would still live,
curled at the banks of the lake
mute as a frond, growing duller

and without distinction.
Her own son had been watching
at the threshold. He had been fine,
and wasn't that fine
for her?
                    When my phrasing stumbled,
she took my place, a mark of artful instruction or
impatience, and sound opened the room, her sound
spacious as escape.
                        I don't know what happened to the boy
or my teacher. Her son lived in the Northeast, visited rarely
and rarely alone. I remember his name,
but not the name of her husband,
who, for years of Wednesdays, opened their door,
his face an austere pallor, calmly nodding
toward the music stand where she waited,
sometimes playing Debussy, her favorite,
sometimes looking out the window.
He'd sit in the kitchen reading the paper
while I played my weekly disasters,
and then, when it was time to leave, he'd walk me
back to the door and wish me well.

Pets

Your grandfather had no teeth
is what I remember best.

                His wife had
hawk's claws for feet, or so they looked,
bound in early girlhood,

        bound till death. She belonged

to the last generation to practice this
warranty for adequate marriage.

              "Adequate" is a euphemism, an
equality knotted at the root: "aequus"

not the "equus" my bad Latin
took me to. In my cantering

thought, a sort of waltz
from daughter to wife,

then dotage: Once a diplomat,

       her toothless husband, our archelder,

now chortled unashamedly
          at my erstwhile guinea pigs.

In his lap, he held George and Charlie,
so jittery with the hasty gut-born anxiety
that makes them want to flee

yet keeps them quivering in place. By then, he'd been
widowed a decade; of his heartache

there was no word. Already

I've forgotten the wife,
your grandmother, my great-.
Her eternal grimace

I read as villainy and not as the beast
of burden she'd been bred to be. I was
the brat, again and again collapsing

all over her broken toes. Your father shook
his head and took his book

to another room.
                        I find it ironic
that your father was a philosopher. His specialty: Taoism,

though he knew his Hegel,
was a shut-in, and had no use for girls:

                        little traps, big mouths.
                        The woman he married

suffered this gravity,
shriller than silence. Forgive me,

I never liked her, your mother (my
        nǎinai!). She taught geography
in provincial Taiwan, could make a jump shot

                even in senility, and cried

when I refused to launder her kitchen rags—
no one had touched her in years—

crying: *wǒ shì ni de nǎinai!*

I did not cry. I was almost no longer a child
so ran out of the house,

as if any world could be had. *What is more important*

than family? you, my father,
ask.

        I have always been a terrible daughter. Or

        an exceptionally good one. I got

that PhD and birthed two boys.
Meanwhile, every story is the same:

you run the books, you run your mouth,
you run the world.

Hydrangeas

I found a dark bird
nestled inside the hydrangea
in the backyard

we were alone
the child I was
and the bird

trembling as if the wind
had crept in with us
but the leaves did not tremble

nor those purple globes
poised over our heads
something was wrong

that the bird could not fly away
despite terror
I could not see

the house from there
could not see brother or mother
who was more scared

the leaves and I
were face to face
and now my sons

do the same in our city plot
leaves to faces
faces to leaves

each finds a space
one smaller
than the other taking turns

disappearing
leaves like giant slapping palms
like plates awaiting bounty

that never comes
what is it about the heads
so many now

blue in the late afternoon
cut off one head
and look

another bursts through
one brother the shadow
of a bird another

waiting his turn
to darken to dwell
every spring I wait

for the flowers
to unfurl open and rage
our hydrangea blooms

white droops by June
my sons my sons
I used to do the same thing

in hydrangeas
with sticks I swirled
the dirt I fell entire

into my own sheer silence
are you hiding from me
or hiding

from each other are you
taking turns being
the bird being the brother

The Death of Socrates

Like Socrates, my father wants to know what we think and why.

So where do I begin?

Yes, the curiosity is genuine, but it is also patriarchal, I suspect.
A glass, a mirror,

I am not.

Lest we forget,

he is the son of a philosopher, and so I

am offspring to reason's offspring.

A daughter—loved despite that.

American—loved despite that.

Socrates has died, but my father has not.

A poet writes an elegy to her living father:

"Your daughter, / I was that ruthless."

Without ruth, is there reason?

Well, I have no ruth. About reason,

I do not know whether there is

any in poetry, though there be ruth. I trace a thread

across the grass. Is it

unraveling from a hem?

Is it raiment from the sky?

Stranger unknotted by night,

worn and barely thread?

If my father has a heart,

it is a spool that holds on

only by turning and

lets go otherwise, other

ways, also turning.

Yet not a wheel, for a spool

goes nowhere, his heart

a place that is no place

I've ever been to, not even

asleep, dreaming, feigning

another life. The thread

takes me in circles,

takes me far, with scarce direction. I live

in stories, captive to

seasons, more trope

than rising action.

Writes another poet: "she has been a prisoner since she has been a daughter."

About which my father quibbles:

"There is the explanation that is put in the language of the mysteries, that we men are in a kind of prison, and that one must not free oneself or run away."

Like Socrates, my father was imprisoned

for a crime he could not help committing.

Drinking the hemlock was of little concern to him
because he stood at the center of history,

surrounded by nodding men; his wife,

weeping operas, torrential arpeggios, torn away

from the prison doors, returned to her mothering,

to a house empty of children.

For years, I, too, wept,

in secret,

and so did not weep at all.

It was from my father

I learned the discourse of better and best.

Which is? When will you be the?

Let there be no definition.

Unlike Socrates, my father is neither upright nor wise.

Unlike Socrates, he is alive.

A Conversation between Women

My friend, who lost her husband
twice, first in death
and then in betrayal, orders
the pinot noir. Outside our window
lemon trees. The loss
she does not speak of—
unable to have children
with a man like that.
                    That she could love him
into her wisdom. Despite her wisdom.
We call that love, the despite-ness.
As if by being senseless, the heart becomes brave.
I think of trees I had
but did not want, the length
of my marriages, what to do
next summer. My other friend,
who decided not to marry,
explains why. We look at the sky
because there is nowhere else
to look. For hours I will sip at my drink,
hazarding clarity, such salt.
                    A teacher once said
there is no place for "because" in poetry
because reasons are not poetic. I wrote
no poems then, though I opened wounds
every day. I want to be alone,
I said to my first husband. I want to be
alone, I would one day say
to my next husband.
                  Without an image,
the teacher intoned, no one will believe
there is pain. His wife hated him, I
observed; she found no pleasure
in any conversation. Oh, I wrote

no poems then. The neighbors could hear
our screaming, mistook it for television
or the trees. Because I hated him
I think of him now.

                    If only that were reason enough.

My Own Private Patriarchy

One father was driving a gold Mercedes-Benz.

One father was listening to the Beach Boys.

One father was having an affair with every woman in California.

One father asked me if I preferred Hemingway or Fitzgerald.

He had never heard of Djuna Barnes, or Jessie Fauset, or Laura (Riding) Jackson.

One father mowed the lawn every Sunday of every summer.

One father wanted another grandson. And another. And another.

One father had a mouth that flattened whether grimacing or smiling.

One father had never before sat on a beach.

Never before had he let the tide rise up and turn the sand liquid under his skin.

Never before had his swim trunks filled with salt and shells, his whole body toppling over with the force of the Atlantic.

One father sat quietly in his cell reading books he once found dull.

This father could make friends even in prison.

One father would dog-ear the last page of the book he'd just finished reading.

One father had been attacked by a cocker spaniel as a child and couldn't stand to be in the same room as the neighbor's beagle.

One father sliced the cantaloupe, the honeydew, a dozen Golden Delicious.

He sliced the Bartlett pears, the mangoes, the papayas, the watermelon, the pineapple we only had at Christmas.

One father washed and ironed his dollars and, for a long time, I thought *This is what money laundering is.*

One father kept a closet full of suitcases, inside every suitcase another smaller suitcase.

One father thought there was nothing better than having another, another, another . . .

One father was afraid to enter the woods behind his house.

One father shelled the peanuts before handing the bowl to his wife.

One father watched his wife eat the shelled peanuts.

One father changed his mind and ate the peanuts himself.

One father had no patience for teaching his daughter how to ride a bike.

How to drive a car, how to tell the truth.

How are driving and lying not the same motion forward, faster and forward, keep going, keep going . . .

One father called Beijing, Hong Kong, Taipei, Busan, Tokyo in the last hours of dawn.

One father had frequent-flyer miles he distributed to his family like the dole.

One father ran five miles every morning in whatever weather the weather happened to be.

One father could say hello in almost every language you'd find in Queens.

In Mandarin, in Cantonese, in Urdu, in Spanish, in Portuguese, in Korean, in Polish, in Russian, in Tagalog, in Chechen, in Fujianese, in Arabic, in Hindi, in Assamese, in Italian, in Hebrew, in Greek, and once he said goodbye in Galician.

One father, for seventeen months, operated the elevator up and down a Park Avenue mid-rise.

One father said he was American.

One father said one day he'd go home again.

One father forgot all his children's birthdays but remembered to pay off his credit card bills.

One father thought freedom was lying or that lying would free him, or he lied again, and I forgave him again, and now we are free and still lying.

One father said good night, good night, I miss you, I miss you.

One father did not say anything, or maybe I never listened to his voicemails.

One father was not the only father I had.

Dialogues (Against God)

how small did you feel

standing on the edge of Bryce Canyon

                    but we are always small

my father turning philosophical again

which is to say wandering away from any self

he might have

spoken of the hour the foolishness

with which we sculpt time into a life

my life is not my life

that I should say I   that I daughter am daughtering

that we think we are different

that we stand on other margins

far from each other the days altering inordinately distantly

to this he sweeps clean my words with the same refutation

but we are always small

which is to say

                        we are as good not here as here

in the static of the hour I call dusk

and he calls dinner

        silence holds its breath

("I'm not dead. Nothing remains, let alone 'to be said'")

it bothered me that he claimed to know my mind

when more often a thought hides like sun in fog

I had asked him for a picture of the canyon

a picture of him against the sky's bluest capacity

was it too much to imagine him standing in enchantment

        did you see limber pine aspen those taciturn
        holier-than-thou trees

        did you see calm irrigation a river a creek and
        farther west

        the ocean and the country of your birth

I did not think you would use a word

like holy he observes from where his voice sits alone

(disapproving and lonely my father)

        what will you have for dinner tonight

        how many times will you circle the block tonight

who will you speak to after me and why tonight

yes I say it all the time

holy holy holy

it does not mean I mean it or understand

An Authentic Life

For most of my life
I did not know or understand
the names of things
I saw every day. Sugar maple, crape myrtle.
I mistook ignorance for wonder,
wonder for grace.

As a child
I watched a friend as she rode
English-style, not knowing
English was not the same as American.
It was a lesson. From a bench

I watched my friend play master,
envied her riding crop, her khaki jodhpurs.

I loved horses
only in theory,
by watching. No horses
hid in my toy chest, no lessons
my parents would've strained
to pay for.

I had not been taught to ask questions.
What is this. Who are you. Why.
I had not been taught to want.

My family was not poor,
exactly. We simply had no imagination
for pleasure.
To us, it was hard enough being American.

Pleasure, as I've learned,
is a will to knowledge. I would never,

like my friend, sit straight-backed
atop a horse. Even in Arizona,

years later, an adult,
I curled into the animal holding me,
overwhelmed.

I was riding Western-style
up the side of a mountain,
the name of which I've long forgotten,

tottering over the ground, over the horse,
over the dust
scratching at my throat.

I laughed into my horse
in what I considered Western style.

When older white people speak to me
they assume I was once a child fluent
in deprivation,
that hardships were endured
to stand before them.

Do they think
she has never ridden a horse,
nor driven, aimless, toward the California coast,
do they think
she has not disobeyed her masters.

Once I watched others ride,
and now I was riding.
That golden memory,
the nights it took

to reach red dirt
and not even see the Grand Canyon.
Was that my deprivation?

That golden memory
of holding on and rising.

—

I read a story about a boy
who'd wounded horses at a stable.
One night, he found them
motionless in their stalls. He was
a groomer or a mislaid luminary. Torn loose
by time, he merely mistook
which animal was in captivity.
I remember thinking

his violence had something to do with
the Latin word for horses, the noun
a crown of meaning.
What looked like equality,
I deemed it so—the horse and I
sharing a kind of understanding.
The horse and I, companionate
if not comparable. Which is to say,

the horses failed the boy
by being neither human
nor wild enough.
The excess of their submission
forming an ache
he had to give expression to.

I did not ride the horse, only watched.
I was a child fluent in deprivation,
wasn't I?

Now that I think of it,
I read the story wrong.
It was not a boy
but a man in the field, and

it was not a horse
but the child of himself
standing astride,

the field relentless, tall grasses
wounding us with their ghostly neighing.

What I remember
keeps happening,

the sun chasing at my back,
the chance to ride
infrequent as freedom,
everyone watching.

TWO

The Innocent

For weeks we watched for hatchlings to come
of three smug eggs tucked into a nest,
the nest tucked into the crook
of a neighbor's honeysuckle. Time nodded,
was nodding—the shred of living, how offhand
the wind teeters toward erosion. Hard at work,
on guard in two backyards, the robins mothered
and fathered their territory daily. And beyond,
our block's alley stretched, aimless as fields,
where watching happens by accident,
by nature. They'd squawk on a streetlamp,
a cedar fence, our back stoop, warning off
the tabby, my two young sons, everyone
stuck at home. I lost my mind with watching
and thought it grief or egotism, the bruise
of yesterday, not least the sky
unraveling another season. It was easy
to mistake the bared skeletal pinions
as lawn clippings, old leaves. That circle
in the grass, a massacre of feathers. That
terrible cat. It was easy to lose my mind.
One neighbor said, Let's not tell the children,
why know the world as always fated
toward remnant. Another said, Go,
take the nest, set it under glass, and make it a lesson.
Instead, I watched our habits pass, the honeysuckle
fade from sickly sweet to nothing but heat.
Call it science. It's summer again, and then
everything's remnant. What did we do those days,
stuck at home, my sons might someday ask. We lived
or tolerated living. We looked away from death.

Children in the World

he cannot sleep
>because he wants a story

he cannot sleep
>so I tell him

the one story I remember
>about my mother as a young girl

how she sat in a rowboat
>a book in one hand

a fishing rod in the other
>we look at each other through the night

with the silence of understanding
>that solitude

is the mind adrift
>is the mind on open water

hoping for a catch
>betting against rain

he cannot sleep
>the light twisting in his eyes

like stubborn stars
>in the dark I follow his eyes

to the lake
>where she is quiet

he cannot sleep
>because he wants to know

what she is reading
            how many pages how many fish

how many times did she escape
            and paddle to the belly of the lake

he cannot sleep
        and I forget there is a story

I was almost told
          my mother at the kitchen sink

her body already dying
          hiding the cancer

it will take years to find
            her body a drought

her body
         a war zone a colony *ilha formosa*

cried the Portuguese sailors
           in the sixteenth century

catching sight of my mother
            uncharted island her memories uncharted as

her body
        years before the rainy season

turned to desiccation decay the grief of a once
                overripe land

now her skin parches easily
            wounds easily now forgotten unknown

he cannot sleep
         already dying she says

never was she happier
                      than as a child in her father's house

doted on by her mother her brothers
                             the neighbor's son

never was she happier
                      the favored child daughter

in the middle of a family
                             in the middle of another century

I cannot fully fathom
                      he cannot sleep

because her happiness is a story
                             is not a story I can tell

An Essay on War

As I do nearly every night,
I will sweep the floor
when my mother dies.
I will miss her and
not call her

and little will change,
like the not-calling. Every night
I think of her and don't call
because the thinking is soothing

and the calling is not. I sweep the floor
and think about what I've been asked
to write, an essay on war.

—

"Most of us have not been to war," I begin,
"yet certain photographs
make us remember
what never happened to us.
Either our imaginations are marked
or no longer our own."

Dust dwelling in corners deforms
what I think of as an edge. There is the wall,
and there, alongside it, trails the dust,
stubborn, unrelenting. There—

a boy asleep on the beach,
a girl turned into flame.
In my mind I am at war
with images, my mother brazenly
unsmiling in a photograph

until the end of time. Her mouth's dark
red, an awful ellipsis. Now, awed
by the body in time, she dons a smile
rinsed out like an absence.
I hate poetry. I hate art. One broad sweep,
and still the house will not be cleaned. My floors.
My nighttime habits. I write
without experience: "Dying is a fact
few of us can bear."

—

My mother is dying and we pretend
nothing will happen. There
is the onslaught. Tiny particles
of my children proliferate . . .
our breakfast crumbs, my grief,
the nothing that scatters across the room,
that won't be swept away. I try
to not burn the toast. I try to not bend
to abstraction, this page
torn out of nothing.
What did you pluck out of the tree?
What did you put in your mouth?

My mother, who is dying,
tells me to lock the doors and windows.
Winter is coming. Every house
is a target. I live
in a house with a writing desk.
As a child, H's mother,

barely escaping the war,
left everything behind—a well-stocked
kitchen, the first books she read in English.
She held on to her
small self, her only baggage,

covetously, terrified
in the back seat of a stranger's car
barreling toward a border.

Now, in America,
my mother is dying. She is scared of deer,
snakes, caterpillars, rats, and some
men. And windows and doors.
I no longer know where she puts the broom,
if she sweeps the house or
answers the phone.

   —

Who made this mess?

I write,

"The mother of all wars
is inside ourselves: I cannot decide
whether to speak or stay silent, or
I speak only ineffectual words,
the crackling sounds that trees make
on a windy night." The season changes; again
nothing is coming out of my mouth.

I read about a family
photograph, the son long gone,
the mother years into a second
language, second life. Her hair is a black wave
in a black ocean. I write,
"Why do we not think of this
as an image of war?" The daughters
look nothing alike.

I am leaving the door open,
the windows unlatched.

I sweep the floor as my children sleep,
I sweep out the leaves
they've carried into the house, every corner,
the dust, the dust, the dust.

My mother was born in a war,
outlasted wars I studied
and wars I never heard of.
Never saw. My whole life.

The Age of Unreason

On January 17, 1989, a young white man entered the schoolyard of Cleveland Elementary School in Stockton, California, with a semiautomatic rifle. He shot and killed five children and wounded thirty-two others. The victims, as well as many of the wounded, were the children of Vietnamese and Cambodian refugees.

when I was a small child
I did dream of murder
a girl named V

who made friends effortlessly
wore purple
and was not unkind to me   not once

I have never told this to anyone
must I identify her race
or only mine   I was small then

as small as those five children
killed in 1989
                    in Stockton California

by an ordinary man
who thought of the shooting
as an expiation

for the loss in Vietnam
for the loss of esteem
for white men   for reasons

that have nothing to do with hate

                       claims the scholar
              standing before us in the lecture hall

it is not personal   in fact there is no feeling
I write it down   *not personal no feeling*
and try to formulate an intelligent question

except I hate
           that I've never heard this history before

and hate that an ordinary man
will somehow find war in anything

and call it valor
call it sacrifice   five black-eyed children
look back at us from the scholar's slide

death lighting their faces eternal
they look like me or worse
like my children

who are playing elsewhere
               in another schoolyard
all our names missing from the pages of history

after interviewing the survivors
the scholar paused his research for ten years
waiting or unable to bear it or the first

draft was a blank page   a silence in the lecture hall
saturated in time

                          silence

outraged by the problem of diction   what word
might begin   what word could

        how do we ask history a question
is not the question I want to ask
and yet I write it down   I remember

about Vietnam   my civics teacher said we won
          I remember   as children
               I did not want to play war

but my brother did   in the woods behind our house
where we found an abandoned shed
the sunken roof revealing a slice of sky

bedsheet soaked in rainwater
no kerosene   two old-time lamps
overturned on the floor

where fungus spawned a kind
of lawn   the mossy walls
the perpetual damp

we had crept in through a window
my sleeve catching on a shard of glass
that once formed a perfect pane   he pointed

to the enemy perched in a silver maple just outside
and my hands became a pistol
aiming at dusk-laced leaves   I am remembering this

in the lecture hall
as I weigh the difference between ruin
and play

                          even as children
we knew the truth
though knew it only lyrically

that some wanted us dead
that marked by difference
we became to some

                        trespassers usurpers an alien pestilence
our very game
               plundered   nothing ours

it is happening
a voice urges another hero into battle
and who's to say it isn't there

the voice the hero or the battle
I cannot see it
                    but I feel it

the scholar explains
it happens every day
and lists the children's names

as if into the majestic field
of a winter schoolyard
they will now march   sons and daughters of war

we were never the enemy
we never lost the war
by dinnertime we were home again

anthems whirling in our heads
knowledge we did not want
            we did not ask who lived here

or why they left or how we knew
                            such emptiness could be ours

what was it that Augustine said   the children
            need a metaphysics
                            we cannot have one

The Lonely Humans

A type of hickory, it grows by water.
So are we fools to drive to the river
the day after our most savage storms
have finally stopped
to see a tree we've never seen before?
To hike in cold mud through a leafless forest,
to behold clearings now cluttered
by whatever fell last night—mostly oaks,
no hickory—to attend the mad performance
of a newly roaring current.
I do not want to call it singing,
the wounded poet's head howling
downriver. Remember we scorned
his broken heart, broken rashly
by himself, some say, for wanting love
too soon. You say I am unfair, that too much
rain is what makes the river rush (*there is no "we"*
in what you say, dear): We hear it
as mythology. We hear it outside
ourselves, a surfeit of music quickening
wind against winter trees, branch-taps
I mistake for premonitions. Of what? That the tree
is here, ready to spring to life again. I am
unfair. I want to love honestly; I want love
honest. Every tree is the wrong tree.
This is the direction we get lost in.
Beech, sweet gum, more oak. But she
was impatient, too, you say, it is possible
she willed him to look back. We do not love alone
is what I think you mean. When I walk behind you,
the back of your head is golden, ungovernable
light I cannot look away from. Is it love
that to follow you I find myself choosing

this unexpected path; should we find the tree,
will it be I who led us there or you? Long gone
are the leaves alternate, compounded, each
an arrow, the thrust of a green thought; somewhere
along the forest floor centuries crack and turn
to dust. We have children, grudges,
a Dionysian mortgage, habits
mostly bad, and yet every December
I imagine spring, our time past
and to come, how when you follow me
I track the blazes to reach the river, and often
I have to stop myself from looking back.
To stay together, look away, some god said.
Here in these trees, our voices have no
faces; we've walked like this for an eternity.

Is Not

Love is not love
is what I read
and what I tell my father

on weekends we talk
there are explanations
how to cook tomato beef

how who we know
got sick who might die
the when untouched yet

always speculating my father
names names resolute
against sorrow is it time

he wonders
to find a new wife
how can I respond

to find alteration
in the monotony
of pandemic time

is not love to read
the tea leaves of her daily
plaint her sleeplessness

her anticipatory grief
as love
is not love

is my mother his wife
irreplaceable mortal
who refuses him

lives two towns away
with another man and
calls my father every day

at dawn a neighbor flipped
onto a stretcher departs
in a parade of sirens

by nightfall forty new cases
confirmed marking our locked-
down day well spent

into the space between
my mouth and the phone
I declare we survived

early in my life
I loved civilization
what I called art

the space between myself
and the world
an ever-fixèd mark

that song is love
that the sky's striation
every wandering blue

the forest a constant chorus
exaltation I thought
truer than my parents

fighting in their room
to the edge of doom
is love

not love is my neighbor
struggling to breathe
breathing

once there was a future
what is art my father asks
it is not love

What Is Truth

The woman in the bed next to mine
was also a wife, also a suicide, and refused
to take off her headscarf.
Both of us had been emptied,
stomachs pumped, hazy,
self-hazed in the bleak hours
before dawn. She had more to say
than I did, more right to her grief,
though our charts read the same,
neither of us content,
neither white. Without my glasses,
the room a yellow blur,
her coal-dark eyes startling
as a reflection caught
in passing. Alone with her,
far from my life, we were
a calm pair, propped up
on white sheets stiffened by daily
bleaching, every touch sterilized,
unfeeling. Like me, she had taken pills:
Vicodin, Percocet, poisoned anapests
choking our throats. She had not chosen
her own life and so endeavored
to leave it—the indifferent husband,
the children, pitiless, pulling at her sleeves,
her hands, pant legs, and hems,
because what body? Her voice hoarsened
by the tube stuck down her throat
to rid her gut of death, now
half cackle, half croak, she mocked
herself, there is no body—
I, too, feel the ache that is all
mind. On the bed beside hers
I was without skin bloodless

boneless worn down by a weeping
that bore no tears. Here, at the threshold
of death's vault, from which we'd both been shut out,
my silence and her voice knocked
at the invisible door.
                              Or am I fooling myself
to think our stories are the same,
our twin suffering on identical twin beds,
two griefs, strangers to each other?
Two women who wake up day after day
done   is a banality.
I have a bounty of friends
I call sisters; none of them know
the truth, that I was dying
in my youth, what one teacher
called salad days then kissed me on the cheek
unbidden. If only I'd told the truth: don't touch me,
don't serve me on the plate
of your sympathy. Oh, it hurt, the process
of being saved. The nurses on the graveyard shift
did not mourn us, their nonchalance
a critique of our dying
and our living. I was not yet thirty.
I did not have to go home,
though I would the next day
because it was easier to hate my life
than to have no home, to commune
in the shadow of a woman
bound to the world as if by law.
I loved her voice, the steely surety of each word.
I loved her voice for not being mine. I believed
that what brought us together was proof
there is no law, only the murmurs
of other women in other rooms, only us
at this late hour in the Western world.

I would be lying if I said those rooms are past.
Now that I am a mother
and no longer want to die,
she is next to me
picking out new words
for pain. Choose this one,
that one, purple blooms
that wipe out the winter, choose
the word that swears we'll survive again.

Dialogues (Against Literature)

Years later I will remember this terrible time as not only about myself

Or not only that to punish my father I made myself unhappy

From my window I could see that much else was wrong

Across the street new construction had struck open an underground pipe, and for months after water would shudder down the boulevard

Not shudder, exactly

It was as if the road had been forced open and was now weeping violently

I had known such devastation in my youth but now

It was happening to the world around me

Summer stretched into November

The chemical clouds I mistook for glory

Benzene flowering overhead like a wild lily

Pinkly iridescent

I thought of my father's loneliness and felt every cell in my body fall silent

And knew this was love

And knew I had come very far in my distance

To let tenderness rule me

Of all the men I despised he perplexed me most

Wretched as Aristophanes and as maddening

Or that professor who shot himself in bed

Leaving a mess for his widow

Whose bulbs I planted one fall when she was too sick to put her hands in the loam

He would lean over me until his beard stroked my skin

Just to say I had misread Cortázar

How one day in my waning thirties I could no longer read Hemingway ever again

"Ever again," a phrase that pains like an early death

In the past my father could choose to forget me and the wounding words we exchanged

And now I forget why I left him behind

Something to do with poetry or risk

That other professor declaiming at a downtown café the need to uproot oneself in order to be brave on the page

As if he ever left his house, as if neither of us had overheard Flaubert flaunting his dull life

Or my father's father, who thought nothing could be better than being his student

Looking around the table accounting for his black-eyed hungry children

All terrible at philosophy

There was only one daughter, who even into her old age everyone described as foolish

Chiding her poor decision to fall in love with a dying man

Though in this she was no vanguard

She held him as he passed, wept the whole of her breath into him, and then the next year sat for days, alone, at her mother's deathbed

And where were her brothers

One was in prison, another in Athens, and the youngest was across the alley eating noodles with a neighbor

Even now my father sleeps through the night and does not dream

On the Soul

after Plato's *Phaedo*

Older now, I open the book
          without fear. My father,
in the other room, restarts

          the electric kettle. And what
is there to fear? Sudden temper,
          a kind of brute exhale

that could belong to anything,
          anyone, until the water boils.
It boils as the self can, overheating

          in talk. In the prison, an old man
awaits the poison that will end his life
          by reminding the listening crowd

that to practice philosophy
          is to practice death, reasoning
that he has always been

          already dying,
the soul's incipient flight   aloft in syntax.
          No tea for me, thanks,

I call out to a voice I still struggle
          to describe—
quixotic, rash, different

          every time. In anger, my mother's name
becomes two huffs of air;
          beseeching, his voice whines,

deflating like a piteous balloon.
        Today I look for mention of the wife,
"Xanthippe—you know her—"

        the sole mention in all of Plato,
and then she's "led away
        lamenting and beating her breast."

Little is known beyond her name—
        "yellow horses," at root—
and her reputation. Centuries later,

        she's still beating her chest, a figure
of comparison for Shakespeare's Katherine
        who's "cursed and shrewd

as Socrates' Xanthippe," or spelled
        erroneously with a Z by Poe.
Perhaps the wife of any notorious man is

        always merely a rumor, and here she is, counterpoint
to reason. Arguing with her,
        Socrates claimed, sharpened

his mind, made him more nimble
        with the most ill-tempered among us: she was good
for philosophy.   So

        a bad wife prepares one for a good death?
What about a bad husband?
                Alive, my father is drinking steam

out of a blue mug. Alive, he asks me
        what I'm reading. An old book from school.
        He laughs and with his free hand slaps away

the air between us.
It's the week before spring.

What do you call those purple things? he asks.

Crocuses,   I say.   An early sign the year's turning
          again.   How to spell?   Crocuses
don't grow where I live now,

          far from my father and my mother,
who no longer live together. Alive,
          he is a chain of questions, a deluge

of questions, a flotilla, a flock,
          aflutter with   questions.   Outside,
it begins to snow. Miles away, my mother abides

the endless rooms of winter. She has never been cold
          and has much to say about
the current state of the world;

          like the snow, she chooses
to stay quiet.   To live
          in constant quarrel is one way

to write poems,   or it's one way
          marriage becomes hearth
to rhetoric.   But what words,

                    what factious discourse,
unabated, made his mind
          a kind of pane to odd and cloudless

light?   I'm not interested in union,
          exactly, but why   we think
we know what we know,

why we make law
of what we deem reason . . .
　　　　　Whose reason?　　　My father has lost

his phone again, and I can hear him
　　　　　opening and closing doors
around his small house,

　　　　　where he lives alone,
where the snow grows so quiet
　　　　　my mother is no longer even possible.

In the story she tells,
　　　　　he was the last young man left in Taipei.
In the story he tells, she laughed at whatever he'd say.

　　　　　For now, he cannot call her,
though he wants her back.
　　　　　　　　　Somewhere I remember reading that

in David's great painting of that scene
　　　　　he began a sketch of her,
weeping at the top of the stairs,

　　　　　leaving her husband behind
with his cup of hemlock,
　　　　　and then with a few pale strokes

blotted her out again.
　　　　　When I look at reproductions of *The Death*
of Socrates, I look at that empty spot

　　　　　and think I see a trace
　　　　　　　　　of her, a history kept at home—
flightless, obdurate, not the soul, and yet not

not the soul,   she is there

      perhaps, if what I read was true,

                if, indeed, I read it at all.

Prodigal

I will not know this street
freely again,

nor the certainty of these trees,
once my primal alphabet,

now uttering tones
I've lost all fluency in.

The thought has passed
before thinking found

a wellspring. First spray
of forsythia, phantom

budding, what explains
the season beyond

words. I used to say
"home" and stayed

there. I loved
the stunning

stasis of my boredom
and heard

lions roaring from
the back door.

No one told me
I could survive

rootless, this
ceaseless wandering

far from the creek,
far from the sparrows.

Once I watched them
scatter together,

their self-made rage
I called music.

Assaulting the honey-
suckle before it could

flower, the artless clatter
of their wings, a ruckus

like violence
rising from the next room.

Every day I heard
their fighting

and in silence
I waited for their fighting

to resume. I thought like a child,
reasoned like a child,

then I put aside childish things.
A patchwork door of rainbowed wood,

weeping that chimed into the night.
This is the home I left.

THREE

Dialogues (Against Philosophy)

after Plato's Apology & in Chicago

I began my education in the *Apology*

and labored over language

that in my head would not cohere

then could not admit to the professor

that within our circle of silence

I understood least

seeking as I was for the spark

of sense

in a philosopher who spoke

ceaselessly and without contrition

"do not create a disturbance"

Socrates warns four times

it is   I think   an appeal to patience

and thus reason

that we must listen

                              for an answer

in the kingdom of reason

I mattered little   this I knew

without any schooling

       —

we moved the mattress to the living room

and watched snow

unwelcome miraculous

one April afternoon

distracted amid midterms

by first love

               this was my education

light vanishing over the Midway

early lilacs bursting impertinently sweet

across the street from Harold's Chicken Shack

years later I still cannot describe it

seasons too indecisive to allow

any difference between skin and wind

the mind evaporating into atmosphere

the bone chill the body must master

living at the edge of a great lake

at the edge of another hard century

       —

mastery was not what Socrates found

in his encounter with the poets

the one detail I remember

with anything like understanding

they were seers or prophets perhaps

yet certainly more ignorant than he

they do not compose with knowledge

                YES   I wrote in the margins

as I said yes to the snow and

one kind of world

                      that might let me in

      —

world of errant weather
world of ponds shaped like lopsided hearts
world of inevitable philosophies
world far from any god's glance
lost world I once imagined as a child
speechless world
Cordelia's world
Josh and Emily's world
world of cold lakes
overdue world
forgiven world
world of silver maples
the weary blues world
world that writes you back
world that loves you back

—

in the living room on the mattress

as my love slept

I found the obituary of a poet

whose obscene incantatory poems

I rarely thought of   too many words I opined

in Contemporary American Poetry   as if I knew better

and then   I was mourning him

was it a good death

                              it had been a good life

so the solemn praise of his friends evinced

up through the third-floor windows

I could still see   snow falling patient and slow

into the sole light of a railroad rental

the steely calm of a still winter sky

dust motes fleeing the cat's steps the pale bloom

of dour clouds   quietly

I lived my life

bound to questions I could not answer

it was April 6, 1997, and the poet was as dead as the philosopher

                              Socrates has a point

there's wisdom in knowing what you don't know

I lived my life

I held the half light

                    and the snow and let everything turn

to glass   myself merely beholding

but sure of love and sure

that what I could not see

namely the future namely myself

was there

                    do not create a disturbance

he warns again

so do I mourn the howling poet

and blame him for the snow

the gray grief of the world refusing another spring

do I neglect to take in the mail to nod

at the neighbor to feed the cat to feed myself

and will I moan like a hungry fool

when the plates are empty

and the milk is gone

I was awake in my solitude

silent as the bookshelves crowding that long-ago room

how often would I lose myself to weather

how often would I know what I didn't know

let the sky finally darken let the snow

ease the rage of sudden stars

A Lunch Date

Across the table from each other
we sat in the nervous light
of our eyes, one

Virginia afternoon, as women might
decide to eat or not eat together.
Everywhere I looked in that town

I could see a house on the hill
where I imagined
we were forbidden. The woman

was loved and possibly
in love, but she was alone in it,
the way any of us can make of coalition

or form
a solitary state. We drank
either coffee or wine, I cannot remember,

bread I gnawed at
instead of speaking my truth,
which was not then in fashion,

and, besides, I did not know it.
I tasted sea salt in the butter.
I tasted local honey.

Why I did not trust her
had something to do with love.
That her portion was different

did not make it more or less
desirable. That she was like me,
another animal studying her corner

and hating it,
did not make me the victor.
Between us

a plate of tiny leaves
heavy with vinegar, our forks
abandoned at the edge

having lost our hope
to share.
                    This morning I am low

in the Hill Country
remembering this woman
I knew briefly. Briefly

a titmouse at the craggy pine,
briefly
the particularity of a face

masking her losses. I remember
we both liked quiet,
inordinately, and agreed

no word could better silence.
It could be otherwise,
I might have told her,

better than loneliness
is solitude, better than love
sometimes. Sometimes that's true.

Dead Ends

The pecan tree outside my window
is an uppercase Y, as if to reflect
that yes, you yawn, you yuck
it up, your yellow-bellied yawping. Or yesterday, or
Yahtzee, the Yangtze River, or it's pure
homophone, the ritual interrogation: why
did I come here, why did I leave
a home I loved?
There are no good reasons
for breaking one's own heart,
though you and I text about it. Now and then,
we observe a death and dole out
ounces of joy—she lived well
or he skipped pointless meetings
flagrantly. The sorrow
is ours alone, living out as we do
a secret faith in time.
We'll die, too, I say.
Maybe, you say.
Yes. Someday.
Time to turn off the light . . .
Outside the hours descend
a decadence of rain, thoughts,
night traffic, this city's rhythmic
throbbing. Consider the first time
we notice a knot in any tree
and see the opening to another life,
unfathomable, complete. More—
consider considering,
that quiet art's astral light,
illuminating from a sky we'll never see.
I should have texted
death is not always darkness. Or
that being far from each other

might permit new radiance.
Now that my eyes are closed,
my body curled into its own warmth,
I dream for you a sublime blizzard.
We should each write a poem
called "Dead End," you joke.
Will it be an elegy? Yes, or an ode.

Yesterday's Myth

When Icarus fell out of the sky,

I was driving my sons to the river.
Mama, what's that?
                                        Bird, I said,

because I couldn't say tragedy.
Too young to understand
the terror

of trusting a parent,
my sons noted wings
like feet kicking at the earth
from the clouds.
                                        We were nearing

the Anacostia, racing along
a ribbon of highway—

                            creature,
                            falling child, is ingenuity
the mistake,
or are you?

                    I think of my father
and the experiment
of his life. He had a faith in fate
that bloomed with age,
his godlike folly, and sang

the ceaseless blaze of the sun. Even now
I swell with love for him,
and with terrible shame.
                            It is too easy

to not see Icarus hit the water,
fathoms deep, culled into
the river's unrelenting rhythms, dead
at best,

              while every father

somehow keeps flying,
even mine. It is too easy
to hide in elegy, pretending I know

what to mourn, as if art were
no accident, as if my sons
weren't screaming
for snacks in the back seat,

each a radius of chaos
that love renames "exquisite"
and "nature." The bird

                 forgotten; the father

and his reluctant acolyte,
both worn out by glory,
are once and for all apart—

                  who am I protecting?

When I fell from the sky,
I was finally free.

A Year

in Washington, DC, & in absentia

I

Evenings I circled a single city block I knew as home,
circled the small plots of oakleaf hydrangea
anonymous without blooms, and I heard
men and women howling from their stoops,
our eight o'clock alarm,
howling like woeful, broken clocks. I heard sirens
racing east on Irving Street,
dissonant choruses singing
the song of the living
and the song of the dead,
imploring us to follow. In the cold impatience
of engines blaring emergency,
in the cataclysm of wolves, streetlamps
light themselves. The yawping
gut, unbearable sound, American marathon
of time, I lived here once
among the increase and diffusion of noise
and called it knowledge.

2

Reading about the city's museums, I learn
James Smithson had never stepped foot
in the country he left his life's fortune to—

which is to say, much might happen
where we are not. Some rooms

hide in grand institutions, some rooms
catch the drafts of
an old row house.

Smithson unlocked room

after room in his mind: some fill
with fortuitous strangers, some lead to a route
beyond oneself, some are waiting . . .

To name myself

I name reasonable wants. I want

coffee. I want to open a new book. I want
a particular thought to pass quickly

before I leave this room
and begin my task,

to endure the day.

Where are you going?

We're out of milk.

The kids could use some fruit. Oranges; it's winter,
after all. Don't forget your mask.

3

In the absence of truth

there must be ginkgo leaves

in the early spring.

There must be labor

in the truth of fine weather.

There must be clarity

to the midday sky, truth

like an open hand.

In the absence of truth,

we dwelled in night

imagined, hale, and almost

true. To dwell in absence,

to dwell without truth—

how can this be home?

There must be a home

in the truth in the curvature

of limestone, in the pink cure of

dawn, where we saw

an orb of steel

spin like first light.

Truth in ancient green spines,

truth in our hawkeyed neighbors,

in the metaphor of taller grasses

now properly raving, truth

in a nest of wires, in vials

of color, in the terminology

of particulate craft—particular

and partial to mystical lyric

machines—that power the humming

of our incidental muses,

what some call spring.

There must be spring

and truth in spring,

and we are measuring

and waiting, and look

how trees can nod,

                yes, the trees are nodding—

    4

A year older, I have come
        to think of rooms

as meadows, relentless seas,
        skies ravenous yet

requiring little. I dreamed I was in a grand gallery:
        the walls turn gold,

and the ceiling rises as a canopy of trees,
        where stray winds twist lush

as drapery, and vaster—
        I can see everything:

masked men and women
        unrolling cloth from the moon,

cloth from another planet.
        They count purple beads

and consider the weather,
        a commons of cumulus and cirrus

clouds colliding.
        They hold up the rafters,

they hold up the moon.
        I had not been ready

for the loss of one life
        and the advent of another.

Wild and sudden flowering
        that was not my heart

but a door opening
        so that I might convene

with a heat not my own.
        How was I to know

this would be the future?
        Before a row of cunning eyes,

I cried *Change me,*
        and so, I was other

than myself, and the rooms
        of my house became a new world.

    5

I understand, the globe might say, as the teacher paces the classroom.

The truth that children know is a question.

Pencils in hands, poised to ask why.

And how. The globe does not spin. A finger pauses
on our country, disquieting as a lion in repose.

What spins?

                              What havoc makes this light?

Letter to Capitol Hill

Dear Daniel,   By the river
you and I might someday stand
two familiarities, friends parted
by place

and time.   Where am I
is a question I'm trying out
daily, but it does not right
the self, nor find me. Yesterday I looked up

a gray bird in a book
about gray birds, discovering
I'd seen it before.
                      Yesterday I found two blue gloves,

like those I'd lost long ago,
palm to blue palm
at the edge of the road.
                 We have never held

hands, though I imagine us
two wizened codgers hobbling
down Constitution Avenue—
             "Put out your hand,

isn't there an ashtray, suddenly, there?"
You know where I'm going . . .
               We circled a park once,
orbiting away from that statue

of a favored president, at his feet
a row of grateful supplicants.
We did not want to get closer
                              but let history hiss at our backs,

wishing each man
stood at his own center, wishing
each man stood as a man.
                              We did not want to get closer,

but I remember the row of their hands
praising or, had we not
known history, pleading
                    for one fair word from another

stone-faced tyrant.
                    I remember walking with you
and remember remembering a certain song,
to "have taught . . .

                    most violent ways . . ." Who is the teacher,
who the student? In school
we loved to use the word "research"
                              as if it freed us from complicity,

as if the archive were not a mirror.
Too soon, you died. Now, heaven, like a nation,
"is the same people living in the same place."
                              You'd say,

"heaven is also a prison." It is a conversation
between what we've read
not what we feel; then who are we
                        and what do we know?

I know your voice
is a kind of heaven. The truth is
your voice doesn't exist
                    even here, this page

that is neither heaven nor nation
but a form   of thinking,
ache, whim, beyond
                reason, and so perhaps better,

what we call a poem: first storm
of the year, winter berries frozen
to the thinnest branches,   new holly trees.
          What to do with this grief?

This letter I never sent?   Please
tell Katherine I read the Catullus
and made her salad.   Again I forgot
the dill. When will I learn?   I write you out of time.

The End of the Story

you gave me all

the woods behind our house, the house,
the art of the retort,

the accounts, the this and that
you deemed love
you gave me the wounds

that became my first
and most lasting teachers

articulating the rot
and the wrong, how to want
more and more—these you gave

by example
rather than handing me

a key

open the door
                        you live here
                                    lived here

in the room beside the kitchen
is a river
into which you step
                        the river is the same

and not the same and you
are you and not you
                    not now not anymore

outside white-tailed deer test the yard's margins

encroaching and then retreat

the deer have learned to speak our language

staking out land as theirs
saying yes and yes and yes

they drink at our river

they corrupt the children

they play the game of time

      I am watching it

the river in the house
the house in the woods

words when I wanted listening

the two of us

father and daughter at the window
asking each other
          what do you see

I am no longer a child
on my hands and knees

pawing the cold wet moss
making heaven of a nearby clearing

      it has been a wet spring

      soon the moss and the hurt will release
      like a breeze   impervious
      green world I run farther into

      green world where I begin   to unlearn everything

Time, Rampant and Flourishing

Certain forests, like this one, invoke
the twentieth century, though this is not a forest

but a city park, land cordoned
for natural recreation—a man-made stream,
black willow trees loved by honeybees, paper-white moths,
and so loved by the wood thrush. Often a trail
is taken
                    with little thought as to where
time leads, what place permits the body
to think and be

                    more, then who measures the centuries and
does a forest conclude?
This one, tucked

                            away like a dream, belongs first to the municipality
and then to a population
                            of white-tailed deer, some say *rampant,*
some say *flourishing.* Once it belonged

to a senator of a western state, who set a small stone house
near that loamy clearing. He found these trees

                            peculiar. Hardwood, deciduous,
not unlike the woman he loved but would not
marry. Why not?
                    It was a different century.

Consider the tree of heaven,
consider the bamboo. What is not native
takes over, and here their roots tangle
underfoot, form an unexpected grove,
an alteration within all this green. The senator's house
has turned now

into a heap of ruin. Otherwise unremarkable,
he was not so prosaic as to wed himself

                            to habit: how easily

being young can be a habit
of being wrong, of writing letters
only to hear one's own voice.
                Love is hard
because who it affirms
is not always the loved one,
           is not always the lover, so what does it affirm?

I never used to care about affirmation. I merely followed
night after night
until one morning I grew tired

of following   and was alone. Does it matter, then,
that the senator never married, dithering instead
                between such mute trees,

which, yes, I may have passed once,
tenderly, and a meadow
        of copious grasses, the names becoming

a secret lexicon, each name   a blade of law. It is a park
or it is a forest. It is older
than any heart.

The Last Horse I Rode

I think of the people
my children will love
of the slow lingering
of a horse in the shade

more wind than woman
I rode out on it once
subject to a direction
I could not determine

I rode farther or rode
not at all a condition I've felt
since young the capacity to be
gone and yet here

I held like weather
adrift atmospheric watching
my children not sure
whether to love or not love

the world meaning
they were not sure
whether to love or
not love themselves

it is not enough to trust
the sky to be parent to this
the rotation of the earth
will not be parent to this

to care is not the work
of the weather
it is not meteorological
it is unkind it is a kind

of hardship to care
we are so lonely right now
when one child was small
he tore papers to pieces

I thought he likes the swift
shriek of a good rip he is
musical I thought he is
strong he tore artwork drafts

newspapers registered mail lists
we wrote to ourselves lists
of promises to each other he tore
a map I'd drawn of a town

we lived in before he was born
he tore apart the past he tore
money actual bills government
forms he tore apart the future

every burden that wakes us
in the middle of the night
awaits him in the morning
he tore it apart and I would

make him repeat after me
we do not hurt we are kind
we do not hurt we are kind
who in this world will love him

who will hold his hand
when he is wrong
        Mama
what are you doing

I am writing a poem
about the last horse I rode
out west across the alfalfa
meadow clusters of sage

my horse stepped gingerly
over the air a luminosity
upon my face the shock
of living that I once believed

would outlast me
what will you think
when we rest hungry
as animals in that dryness

what the poet in me wants
to describe as sere what will you
admit when the people who
will someday love you ask

if your mother sang to you
if her words brought comfort
what silences did she lay out
in the tall grasses looming

taller striving to become
more meadow the plenty
you will never understand
until it is gone if the world

could not love you back
if your mother could not say
hush how often must I
open the window

and not know and not
see the sere the searing
that the sounds we could not
call human are human

my children you must love
in kind the world the people
you must kindly love
the rain eroding another

weekend the flowerless
late fall hickory bark and
acres of treefall and then love
the rain not coming at all

Notes

All quotations of Plato are from G.M.A. Grube's translation, *Five Dialogues: Euthypro, Apology, Crito, Meno, Phaedo.*

"The Poem of Force" uses language from Simone Weil's "The *Iliad,* or the Poem of Force" and John Keats's "On First Looking into Chapman's Homer." Brian Blanchfield once suggested that we each write a poem after Keats's but about reading Emily Wilson's Homer. This poem is the best I could do, and it is for him.

"In the Middle of My Life" is for Cecily Parks, who walks with me.

The quotations in "The Death of Socrates" are from Natasha Trethewey's "Elegy," Louise Glück's "Persephone the Wanderer," and Plato's *Phaedo.*

The quotation in "Dialogues (Against God)" is from Frank O'Hara's "Death."

With regard to "An Essay on War," I must thank the editors of *Paideuma* for giving me the assignment and sincerely apologize for never completing it.

"The Age of Unreason" concludes with a misquoting of Frank Bidart, who wrote "Confessional": "Man needs a metaphysics; he cannot have one." The attribution to St. Augustine is an intentional error. The poem was inspired by a lecture delivered by Eric Tang on April 6, 2022, for the Center for Asian American Studies at the University of Texas at Austin, and is also indebted to the Foundations of Asian American Studies seminar taught by Ida Yalzadeh and organized by Yanyi in the summer of 2022.

"Is Not" references Shakespeare's "Sonnet 116."

An obituary for Allen Ginsberg appeared in *The New York Times* on April 6, 1997, which is referred to in "Dialogues (Against Philosophy)." In Chicago, where the poem is set, although lilacs had begun to bloom, it snowed heavily on that day.

"Dead Ends" is for Daniel DeWispelare, who asked me to write it in the first place.

"A Year" uses language from James Smithson's papers and Randall Jarrell's "The Woman in the Washington Zoo." An earlier version of "A Year" was commissioned by the Smithsonian Institution for their 2021 annual report to accompany Stephen Voss's photographs documenting the closing and reopening of the institution's museums and research centers during that pandemic year. I am grateful to Lawrence-Minh Bùi Davis, the editorial staff at the Smithsonian, and the team at Polygraph for their support throughout the writing process.

"Letter to Capitol Hill" uses language from Frank O'Hara's "For Grace, After a Party," W.B. Yeats's "No Second Troy," James Joyce's *Ulysses,* and Ralph Waldo Emerson's "The Poet."

About the Author

Jennifer Chang is the author of *The History of Anonymity* and *Some Say the Lark,* which received the 2018 William Carlos Williams Award. Her work has appeared in numerous publications, including *The American Poetry Review, The Believer, The Best American Poetry, The New Yorker, A Public Space,* and *The Yale Review,* and has been honored with fellowships from MacDowell, Yaddo, and the Elizabeth Murray Artist Residency program and with the Levinson Prize from the Poetry Foundation. She is the poetry editor of *New England Review* and teaches at the Bennington Writing Seminars and the University of Texas at Austin.

Poetry is vital to language and living. Since 1972, Copper Canyon Press has published extraordinary poetry from around the world to engage the imaginations and intellects of readers, writers, booksellers, librarians, teachers, students, and donors.

WE ARE GRATEFUL FOR THE MAJOR SUPPORT PROVIDED BY:

academy of american poets

OFFICE OF ARTS & CULTURE
SEATTLE

ARTSFUND

THE PAUL G. ALLEN
FAMILY FOUNDATION

Hawthornden
Foundation

POETRY
FOUNDATION

INGRAM
CONTENT GROUP

the point
envision·enact·evolve

McSWEENEY'S

WASHINGTON STATE
ARTS COMMISSION

National
Endowment
for the Arts
arts.gov
ART WORKS.

The Witter Bynner Foundation
for Poetry

TO LEARN MORE ABOUT UNDERWRITING
COPPER CANYON PRESS TITLES,
PLEASE CALL 360-385-4925 EXT. 105

WE ARE GRATEFUL FOR THE MAJOR SUPPORT PROVIDED BY:

Anonymous

Jill Baker and Jeffrey Bishop

Anne and Geoffrey Barker

Donna Bellew

Will Blythe

John Branch

Diana Broze

John R. Cahill

Sarah J. Cavanaugh

Keith Cowan and Linda Walsh

Peter Currie

The Evans Family

Mimi Gardner Gates

Gull Industries Inc.
    on behalf of William True

Carolyn and Robert Hedin

David and Jane Hibbard

Bruce S. Kahn

Phil Kovacevich and Eric Wechsler

Maureen Lee and Mark Busto

Ellie Mathews and Carl Youngmann
    as The North Press

Larry Mawby and Lois Bahle

Petunia Charitable Fund and
    adviser Elizabeth Hebert

Suzanne Rapp and Mark Hamilton

Adam and Lynn Rauch

Emily and Dan Raymond

Joseph C. Roberts

Cynthia Sears

Kim and Jeff Seely

Tree Swenson

Julia Sze

Barbara and Charles Wright

In honor of C.D. Wright
    from Forrest Gander

Caleb Young as C. Young Creative

The dedicated interns and faithful
    volunteers of Copper Canyon Press

The pressmark for Copper Canyon Press
suggests entrance, connection, and interaction
while holding at its center
an attentive, dynamic space for poetry.

This book is set in Garamond Premier Pro.
Book design by Phil Kovacevich.
Printed on archival-quality paper.